love in a dry land

love in a dry land

Dennis Cooley

TURNSTONE PRESS

love in a dry land
copyright © Dennis Cooley 2024
Turnstone Press
Artspace Building
206-100 Arthur Street
Winnipeg, MB
R3B 1H3 Canada
www.TurnstonePress.com

All rights reserved. No part of this book may be reproduced or transmitted in any form or by any means—graphic, electronic or mechanical—without the prior written permission of the publisher. Any request to photocopy any part of this book shall be directed in writing to Access Copyright, Toronto.

Turnstone Press gratefully acknowledges the assistance of the Canada Council for the Arts, the Manitoba Arts Council, the Government of Canada through the Canada Book Fund, and the Province of Manitoba through the Book Publishing Tax Credit and the Book Publisher Marketing Assistance Program.

The epigraph on page vii is from the essay "The Poetics of Rita Kleinhart" published in *A Likely Story: The Writing Life* by Robert Kroetsch in 1995. It is used with permission.

Printed and bound in Canada by Friesens.

Library and Archives Canada Cataloguing in Publication

Title: Love in a dry land / Dennis Cooley.
Names: Cooley, Dennis, 1944- author.
Identifiers: Canadiana (print) 20240458214 | Canadiana (ebook) 20240458222 | ISBN 9780888017833 (softcover) | ISBN 9780888017840 (EPUB) | ISBN 9780888017857 (PDF)
Subjects: LCGFT: Poetry.
Classification: LCC PS8555.O575 L68 2024 | DDC C811/.54—dc23

for Diane, Dana, and Megan

"We write as a way of inviting love. Each text is a request that says, please, love me a little."

—Robert Kroetsch, "The Poetics of Rita Kleinhart."

Contents

I.

June 22, 1932 / 5
unsparing / 6
secretarial / 7
shipwreck / 8
bright shining as the sun / 9
the abasements of love / 10
they step into the night / 11
les mouches / 12
bramble bush / 13
phantom pain / 14
gardeners / 15
dragging them out / 16
hands out / 17
dream beds / 18
Nefertiti / 20
children in winter / 21
New Year's Eve / 22
June 14, 1933 / 24

II.

on the road again / 27
Philip at the easel / 28
the prophet / 30
graphite / 31
dry-land farming / 32
she imagines him / 33
how it goes / 34
stubble burning / 35
Sunday guests / 36
visitation / 38

Philip's train / 39
a bottle / 40
a matter of debate / 41
he studies the masters / 42
Philip reconsiders his sermon / 43
wanting to know / 44
church: portrait / 46

III.

Paul's sign / 49
El Greco again / 50
Paul, bodacious / 51
calling Paul / 52
school reader / 53
home and school / 54
art class / 56
a light shower / 57
jalopy / 58
changelings / 60
rustlers / 61
the sound in my heart / 62
she contemplates meeting / 63
summer fair / 64
goin' down the road / 66
she invites him in / 68

IV.

soufflenheim / 71
he thinks of her / 72
misgiving / 73
caesarian / 74
sparrows / 75
last days / 76

prophecy / 77
cattle in winter / 78
amaryllis / 80
every tuesday / 81
renunciation / 82
here & now / 83
she has scanned / 84
the back step / 85
eremite / 86
she rejoices in her days / 87
the air strangely dead / 89
the days unfold / 90
small birds / 91
dreamt of you / 92
what I wanted / 93
she gets ideas / 94
Christmas Eve / 95
travelling salesman / 96
unreturned / 97
voilà / 98
windflowers / 99
Closed Until Further Notice / 100

V.

small laugh / 103
killdeer / 104
the small flowers / 105
hearing your name / 106
pebbles / 107
we draw our breath / 108
concert / 109
in what of you / 110
she poses / 111

prodigal of dream / 112
radio active / 113
Judith / 114
snowblind on a siding / 115
missing person / 116

VI.

a hurricane of wind / 123
the pebbles clack / 124
she bides her time / 125
skittish / 126
end of the day / 127
if it is true / 128
she hides her face / 129
she is wounded / 130
somewhere near Lampman / 131
wouldn't stop / 132
the itch / 133
for their needs are strong / 134
under the trestle / 135
they meet in the night / 136
they meet in rain / 137
the weight of our clothes / 138
want that / 139
recital / 140
copyrighted / 142

love in a dry land

I.

June 22, 1932

Dear Mom,

Just a quick note to assure you.

Have a bit of sewing on the go—a blue plaid cotton, tolerable in a minister's wife but best of all comfortable for summer. Some curtains for the windows, blue, pinstripes. I hope to brighten the place a bit.

But it's off to supper. Why I feel it's some kind of final reckoning I'll never know, Philip never minds. The clock talks to itself all day long, and I do too, and then it's five and it's talking to me, I'm all ears.

Please say hello to Aunt Ellen and Uncle Fred. I will write them an anniversary letter. Hope you are feeling well and can get into town soon to see us. Same to Dad.

Take care. You know you are always near my thoughts.

My Love,

Phyllis

Philip wants me to remember him to you.

unsparing

that's me: prodigal of dreams
and would-be profligate with today
i take heart in maybes and hope
to coax a little out of life
i'd splurge on chlorophyll if i could
if i knew how and were a cow

it's thrift and theft and fingers in the way
a savings box tighter than a collarbone

until he blushes   naturally   as he would
being a man of the word

meanwhile the parson's wife
pursuant to the town's edicts will
flinch and sour with disappointment
seek solace in penury

she must say no to allure and why not
until at last she or at least
the seventh seal is broken

secretarial

what is this   journal
why am   i   writing always
scratching &

what do   i scrawl   who do i
write to   why do
i do this

i know we must
swallow our words whole
close our throats to saying

this is love in a dry country
this is love in our house
this is the country i take down
careless with blot and erasure

it is the place we live in
and don't dare say

shipwreck

by night the tall houses they call elevators
  grow stark & blind
    darkened by storm
the entire country washes ashore
to burn or heal in salt

look for me in a blood-red sun
in the rusted spores in my hair
turning to sea weed
    pulling us down

day is a squeezed lemon
our eyes are going white in the sun

bright shining as the sun

the days we scold
are never enough
to hold one another
over the stove until
one of us is scalded
and one of us satiated

we know all the men
and all the women
who have been there
ten thousand years
are turning to rock
earth pressed hard against them
their eyes scaled over
mineral and unblinking

the abasements of love

he huffs & sneezes
digs with a fury
digs with protean zeal
to bury or to excavate

he is a flurry of dogness
and he flings the dirt behind
to please i suppose and appease

unsure of provision or of faith
he devotes himself to a bone hoard
    crouches for a word
knows how simply things can fall in
    and come undone

they step into the night

when the horizon breaks open
it will ooze blood, the night will swell
to an animal that is close and sweating

a thick placenta i could live or die in

i will send feelers,
something waiting, wanting something,
the lamp in my hand smoking

the night flops at my ankles,
in the back shed the horse shifts and rubs,
          looks up, expectant

     what am i doing here

les mouches

in April the black birds
are swaying on cattails
open in the wind
like letters from you

in summer the insects speckle
pieces of silk like small flies
in dots, diamonds, stars, moons,
no help for my scars or
my own imperfections

even the shiny beetles
hard black buttons in the hand
seem astringent as stinging nettle

when i try to answer i can feel
the fishbones stuck in my throat

bramble bush

you will forgive the fabric
of shade and verandah
flimsy as a neighbour's curtains fraying
when the world calls by unbidden

if we could keep ourselves
the tight stiches in Egyptian cotton
inured to thread-bare

"baumwolle" the man announces
that's tree wool and there is the tree
in which lambs were caught

in the next life he says we will be
balls of the purest cotton
or, as likely, mats of wool
snagged on gossip and
torn on impossible dreams

phantom pain

             Abe Jarvis says
        it aches   all the time
          day in and day out
never fail, especially when it rains
all the way to the tips he doesn't have
he waves his three-fingered hand

you too Philip
          i can feel you
        to the very end
to the tips of my body
             when you are
          not there

it hurts all the time
          the soft places
     where bones were

      i can feel you
             not there

gardeners

all winter you husband your pain
fill your pockets with it

you pick & sharpen sticks
to note the seasons and to mark the rows

when you hammer in the stakes
you will attach the names that call the seeds out

the seven planets will jostle
and wobble spring loose

come summer you will water your hurt
and you will weed the small places of joy

your plans will flap and crinkle in the wind
ghosts you mistake for pillowcases

why not in the morning return
to what is left of the rows
in wind and snow and the fallen twigs

ðragging them out

the dried thistle a fine brocade
i fuss over little pieces of life
ferret and dribble them

i commit to the earth
bless it with minerals
with my spit split open
the spirit in them

i am after a few carrots
and potatoes if lucky
faint hope for cabbage i know
same for corn or pansies
you can forget it

yet the odd fuchsia pips
a waxy red and purple
dangles from a hanging pot

if it were a carnation
that's it for caution
i'd nip it, quick,
jab it straight onto
his dumbfounded heart

hands out

beneath a sour sky
the only signs of life

they scratch for grass pry for seeds
so precious they could be taken
for wonders in the pharaoh's granaries

they have learned they are fugitives
and are liable to snares and slingshots
homeless little men
worn by grit and heat

they enter the small villages of the barely living
and those of the dead where they fan out
rummaging for food

sun-dried hoboes who must perform
tricks beneath a sun that shrinks
every blade with its breath
pulverizes the kernels to chaff

the wind pours mournfully
the sky turns black
turns its back on
the little men, refused shade,
who stand in the wind & heat
                , hands out,

    „waiting

∂ream be∂s

the man from the university
says they are dream beds
the Assiniboine would lay in
small pits they would hollow
in the hillside & lie in
just below the wind

the sun finds me clearing away the dirt
a rabbit white with winter
snow still coarse in the brush
and a chill on the air

i close my eyes.
      & open them.
           & dream.

could be a cradle could be
the word the earth speaks
when it is remembering
the stiff wind and the blowing.
the scatter of birds
& no one in sight

earth beneath my back and
the warm breath on my face until i am thawing
a crocus in a small gasp breaking through and

                                      /a dog
only it is El Greco and i am back in
the matted grass, the thick smell

                    me and a man
in a long dark coat saying
    what am i doing here
    what am i doing

Nefertiti

i am not myself
at the bottom of a desert
but there was the woman
who dandled six daughters
and held her face to the sun

when the man whose head her head was in
vacated his workshop and fled
like a camel with scorched feet

she fell into the ground
and hid on the other side
eased into the dark earth
where she slept forever and never erased
never lost her beauty or her one good eye

in the end must have given herself up
and come back from the dead

children in winter

imagine myself
the lines neat as a teacher's
on the black board

children who run behind
their clouded breath, shouting,
the bright lives they chase
snow spraying their faces
their mitts clog with ice
and leaky noses

the runners they jump on
and squatting ride
inured to caution and injury

all the children i never knew
laughing and running behind

New Year's Eve

snowed in at the Aberson's
a winter conflagration

can hardly remember
when last i saw you
or think when i do
what to do, how begin,
keeps me here
face pressed to the pane

spend the morning blowing on a forest of frost
trying to snuff out a few trees
burning them off with my mouth
     an ellipsis of watching
     the white window
     the road so long
     it spares nothing

certainly not me, shabby missus to the reverend,
frumpy as the rug slung over the door
cold leaks through and around
the flimsy curtains and the coffee pot
long having called it quits
and ceased its perking

not a sleigh in sight, not a coyote
     or the slightest shift in the fields
       not even a skiff of snow

the sky is hammered into place
over an aluminum road
the mailman if there were
one would come up the lane
lugging in huge barrels of breath
smacking his mitts for warmth

    she, knowing,
busies the silver she has already buffed
shines the room with her breath

      and the man bursts in from the barn
    hauls in big armfuls of cold
red-faced and stomping
happy new year he calls

        ,,looks up, for a moment,
          then away and i am
            grateful for the tact

June 14, 1933

Dear Mom,

Got a minute now, Philip's taken Steve to the ball game, Steve pestering till he did.

Remember I was telling you about the piano? Well there is other news. Judith West, such a pale young woman. Philip tells me I am silly to think of a flower but I do and he says have I heard her sing? It's true. A wonderful voice, you would envy for the choir, and that's counting the Harris girl and her lessons. It reaches right inside, something you knew but never heard. There's a kind of loneliness, almost, in her. You'll laugh, but I think of home when she sings. All wind and yearning.

I've been toying with the idea of playing with her, if she liked —the two of us spiffied up. The Robins of Arcola. They'll be talking about this clear to Sintaluta.

And then there is Paul Kirby—a short man, he teaches, and he's full of ideas. I think I mentioned him last time. He's quite all right as far as Philip's concerned and I'd say Paul feels much the same about him. A wife's pride, I know, but there it is. I'm sure he'll call by.

And then there is the garden. Not much of a garden I'm afraid. Potatoes, peas, beans, carrots—a few things I scratch away at. Phyllis the hen, that's me. It won't amount to a hill of beans, this year at least, forgive me mother, but it is something. Parsnips for The Parson.

I would love to turn out one of those gardens you always had, when the potatoes jumped out of the ground like gophers. One of these years it will happen, just you wait, and there'll be pickling like there never was before.

Flowers too— Geraniums maybe—

Love,

Phyllis

II.

on the road again

The tin can shakes out of the garage.
Rattles like a rainbarrel full of rocks.
Shakes with anticipation.

It will take us to Paul's for lunch.

Talk about luck.
We can't believe our luck.

Philip leans over and hammers the horn.
Arrghghhgghaahh! the car says

likes it so much it speaks again
Aahhrrghuuga ahh

rrruugggaah

the joy half choked in him
Phillip blushes and squeezes the wheel

Aahhhrrruugghhaa!

guides his big goofy grin
clean out the door

Philip at the easel

                  he reaches up /**whump**
                    pulls the sky down
           he is showing
the LATEST ATTRACTION
or coming /he is not sure which
but movies will appear in technicolour

smiles as he rinses the dust off
watches himself as he brushes
a box of cobalt into sight
and under it earth becomes
a wedge of green he turns
the fields under his hand
shiny in grass and water

and over that or in it he spatters
a patch of intense yellow
dabs a softer blue wisps of white
over it all and above it
a white cup of light

grins sheepishly when he says it's pastoral
it brightens a corner in our lives
adds small greens, yellow spots
frogs, he says, when he sees my face

          since when i say
forever he says or seems to say
                    \and there they are
their voices in arcs from their throats

the old show-off he is doing
his best to fill the ark
he says and he
reaches just behind
one swift stroke and there it is
a quick string in the grass

               just in time
               just before dark

the prophet

everybody could see
the hauling wind
the howling sun
one long abrasion

he could feel the land
with its bad stitching tearing apart
the neighbour's tut-tutting
the hard scar we might ride
somewhere near to where
we might almost be us again

graphite

consider then
this my man, P.
is not he faultless
without blame or blemish
immune to slight
when he bears with me
my unspoken anguish

what can be said of his silence
when he bends at the paper
and his hand limbs
the edges of sorrow
whisks what's left onto the floor

he shadows the wet-ash flame in me
a sadness he sees
but cannot say

ðry-lanð farming

no pretending he is not cramped
in the collar he wears
and does not cough
like a draught horse
that he is not burnt
like a loaf of bread

he has dragged forward & versus
in a row with god the words
he has read but does not believe
until they rose in a cloud
and blew with the grasshoppers

he is on his way to meet
his maker or at least someone
who will come undone and wake
the water from the ground
or shake it from the air

she imagines him

we shall come rejoicing
and the world will surge at his feet

a land-locked sailor totters
as though he can
hardly keep his feet
believes in sheaves & eve's
wet-ear speech

resist he says we must
resist all that is that is
bedeviled with spring
the cool soft mist
we should fear rain, resent water
it will only turn to rust

he looks bewildered looks out
as if he were a horse
head-shy from being struck

looks for something to blunt the surprise
somewhere to bed down for the night

how it goes

wish i could tell you
how it is, the confusion,

it will crash like a piano
and splinter on the sidewalk
it's an old comedy, of course,
everyone hears, no remedy,
and no one is ever hurt,

and in gentler times
the shade of a poplar
the smile you stepped into

and the times it shakes
across the roads, like a torch,
certain to boil over

how it goes when i spot you
on the rim of yesterday
on the horse you have ridden
to find me at the correction line
with a wave and a jar of ice

stubble burning

you stoke the rumbly old furnace
you call your conscience
what about your alkaline breath
what about our own warty souls
that shrivel in dust

and yes it rains lickety-split
fire from heaven and you
carry your bowl of dust with you

we know we are scabby bushes
and we are consumed
along the ground and before you
know it we will have become
trees and swallowed

it's a perfect time
it's high time
we made a move

play this right and
we shall be
glowing red hens
and singing real pearl buttons
in the Saturday movies

Sunday guests

paring potatoes for supper and
we are having guests, yes,
         and he is
      coming he will

appear and i am leaning into
the smell from the cellar
some with warts and cuts
where someone stabbed them

the white filaments have burst
out of the leathery skin and thrown
eyes through the damp
they squint and grope toward others
faint purple, pale yellow,

they feel strange in my hands
bruised at the sockets
when i am cutting away
their almost sour taste

i am waiting for Philip
who is in the study
with the membrane of pipesmoke
he tucks himself in
the sturdy bend to his thoughts
grained as oak and as hard
or so to me it sometimes seems
his mind stained with tobacco
from wanting to be worthy

i am at the wet pile of skins
the old potatoes in my hands
lopping off damaged parts
feeling for bad spots
gouging for their pink eyes

visitation

he is a clerk at the wicket
working something wicked
he has been saving against loss
and has dragged it shut
a cliché against wind and forfeiture

Philip who has passed through
the garbage of our neglect
across the last cabbage patch
and through the broken gate
is disappearing into the fence
a pale glimmer in dust

with a sudden yank directs the Model-T
through its creaks and protests

heads for a knuckle of light
in the Macleod window
someone sick and dying
under a yellow vigil

      no idea when he gets there
      what he could possibly say

Philip's train

a cold hard eye
in the darkness is
feeling its way
the terrible beauty

it chases the eye torn
from its forehead
the strange round body churning
its grasshopper legs

would hope to show
how it rustles the curtain
and shrieks at every crossing
the sudden screams when it senses
it is closing on something

when it arrives
sits back on its fat haunches
taking in the darkness
talking to itself

in long black gasps
hush hush it says
HUSHHUSH

a bottle

Philip takes it by the throat
looks past as if something
i cannot sense were there

at least he is not
shooing flies from the saskatoon pie
he took from the oven to count the crimps
that is my tart and brown-sugar heart

or me waiting on the bench
bathing suit sticking
to every grain of eternity and

out he comes with the glass
accompanied by St. Paul
a round and buoyant genius
him and his comic-book speech
more sparkling than ice in soda

a matter of debate

no oh no he says
it's always a quarrel
    with himself

listen to this
the man is saying listen

he tries reasoning
but then he loses
all the arguments
it's one embarrassing rejoinder
    after the other

all his debtors and all
his detractors turn on him
they are skilled debaters
and they unnerve him
release the speed in link & conjecture

when he sees my consternation
he says well that's it isn't it
he always gets in
the last word
the other guy

he studies the masters

The world is smeared he says
never plaintive as people suppose.
You can hear him breathing as he stirs
a speckling of dust he is
a small furnace blowing
grit onto the horizon in the best
cosmic or cosmetic fashion
making the very latest & oldest.

Until we come out from behind the curtains.
He is placing us in places we can lead our lives,
perform before the world
goes its way and there is no time.

People will envy the forces wound in us.
Philip will see wounds in the air.
He will turn toward us a small green eye.

Philip reconsiders his sermon

as for and seed were forth the days, grass, night; kind. let the night; upon And let earth: night; earth: in firmament kind, fruit kind, be brought from herb and for that and whose of And be in the fruit after earth: of seed the yielding the after and kind, herb night; And after so: in after earth: earth that the tree and fruit saw was seed, and whose yielding third so. earth whose years: kind, saw day. yielding good. fruit night; yes after evening evening fruit, from

wanting to know

porch empty
the sitting room
vacant as a Bay
Street conscience

cabins closed and those behind
thinking vagrant thoughts, or not,

the others at the pavilion
where you waited
burned down the music
into dust and ragweed

the ball game rained out
and i suppose i should
think of it as a blessing
a miracle at least

a very hard storm
exhilarating in a way
big dark clouds shoving

and it rained.
\really hard,
the rain driving in sideways

how hot it was
day after day, and those huge moons,
deer so still among the hills

i was hoping to speak to you
wanted to say something
wanting to know you might hear

church: portrait

just this once it is a ship
small and fragile in a brown sky
he swipes a granular wind
on the canvas adds a gray
farmhouse off by itself
where it is pinched to the bottom,
stars, darkness, a pale-thin moon

a big-boned man standing beside
could be the lost Finn on his way across
the man's eyes are squeezed shut
from too much not travelling
from too long in the sun
or so it seems to me
       too much wind
          too much salt

touches with the pointed brush
there and there and there and
a dozen lights so small
you can't at first tell
pop open in the night

the church on an enormous sky
rides out the wind
a wooden grasshopper in august
a ship rattly with rectitude,
the air loud in our ears

III.

Paul's sign

crayoned on the door
he shows the world

> the word is out
> side the door
> out of order

an N-try

> try N it
> shall be O
> pen to you
> say yes
> yes it is
> a bit prim

LM
entry

Airy the 1st

> thing you notice the A
> BC of things AD
> also in it i
> ally you too do this
> is where you are
> this is where
> you start it
> all beg ins here
> the inns have it
> in deucing inte
> rest before all
> others Grade One Pro
> duce A-1 Hard A- all the way

LM
LM
entry
entry

El Greco again

night on the front porch
the pooch the moon and i
afloat on a patch of light

would you look at that El Greco
i say scratching his ear
yes the one that's not there
what do you say boy, hmmm

the garden is drinking
the moon is towing a million
angels perhaps even all of Los Angelos
Paul in his best Spanish accent has proposed
we are beached on the shores of eternity

El Greco who would prefer to be
mauling his bone hoard
the one he never had
in the dark has turned sceptic
    more than willing to mooch
        snuffs snuffs
                noses for scraps
    and a little love

Paul, bodacious

i cld tell he was hot under the collar
the minister who calls on
the parishioners who think he's got me
so buttonholed i could fill cisterns with my grief

truth is i have collected hurts in a cannister
and my wishes in stone jars under the stairs
way down at the bottom among the sealers
i know where they keep
the warm and coloured buttons

        i also know Paul
        is staunch as a ranch
        and devastatingly spiffy
        a kenspeckle charm
        in shirt studs and cuff links

        he speaks so deliberately
        he could be
        a gold assayer and i for him
        so sparklingly new i could
        pass as a jeweler in eaton's

calling Paul

sometimes i call him Paul
sometimes when he is on the road
and he hits the dust full throttle
you have to wonder
why scuttle our dreams
                what is this
          epistle to the Ephesians

i guess he is not to be
caught ought to be hot
footing it to paradise
and sometimes he is not
very friendly sometimes

when i call him he does not hear
some times i call him up
some times i don't call him at all
the right times or places

            he moves in thirst
            speaks like an apostle
            wire brush in his throat

& some times i am done with him
   & do not call him at all
  sometimes i call him names
some times i do not call him at all

school reader

gray cover on the big fat reader and in it
a story of calloused angels who
spit on their hands **smack smack**
they chew on the ankles of trees
and whack the shins from under them

the pioneers held torches to their feet
they had breathed their last, the trees,
and the forest crashed in great sighs around them
offered up their corpses in belching smoke

        a small voice, its wonder :
please teacher were there really
                    /trees
and well why would they
      want to
              kill them   i mean
wouldn't they just sit under them
  all the people there
    where it was cool,
           and birds
and moms and dads

home and school

mothers at the back, watching
small children, and big, restless

chalk dust and wax paper sweet-rotten smell
apple cores and bologna and leaky noses wet mittens
steam on the radiator which clanks as always it has

we lean into the stories and the dribblings of erasers
the little cries the desks let out
the insects that brighten in the seasons
which if anyone scratched would burst into fire

the smells swarm the desks
whose hearts promise and arrows confess
the kids have cut their secrets
the letters stained in deep-ink devotion

behind me on the board
a kid's strokes of suspicion
a figure in frizzled hair, yellow-orange,
a face full of eyes, large and loose,
and magnified to bed springs
TEACHER'S GIRL it says and it
adds a short man, TEACHER, book in one hand
love in a dry land it says
in big letters on the cover

at night there will be
birds pecking at the stars
thick as thistles, as abiding

oh send me letters Paul
          send me
   epistles to the heathens
        and you,
              you could call me
   any time

art class

and who is this Ryan
that's Mrs. Bentley, teacher

        Paul looks up,
catches my eye when i see
my mouth a slash of crayon
wide as a canyon i expect and
eyes big as drawer pulls

i can see my nose
is a shoe and it seems to have
fallen out from under a bale of hair
messy as dreams and walking
in its own directions

enough of this
enough of this face whisked
by the straw-broom hair and
what looks also like cyanide eyes
a face throwing off splotches of alarm

a boy named Ryan has come
all the way from Sintaluta
and he would if he dared
wire a tiara of sun over me
glowing as Beehive Golden
Corn Syrup on a barn door
plus startled bits of glass
that brighten my eyes

a light shower

the soft & sudden rain
releases the heady aroma
the warm curtain of flesh

petrichor he reassures me
the smell from the wounds of the gods
the mineral exhalations

i wait where the hail arrives
and the screen door slaps

it is always blowing
I am always alone

everything swims or stumbles
every creature comes to drink
and some to cry out

jalopy

1.

Paul hunches over
the wheel small
bear at a honey pail
eases the spark
retarder bumps
the lever and Philip
at the front fearing
he will be erased
or left in the dust

the dust hits
as if someone had
thrown a blanket of sand
our faces and hands so dry
we might have been picking potatoes

and the car shakes noisily awake

2.

you revel in the geometries your car takes
as if sent to renown on the side of the road
                    to a flat and no jack

you peddle yourself in glory past the horizon
with a red bandanna at your throat
and an indecency or two cantering
into the country and the sun bouncing
jauntily on our shoulders

an organ thumps and wheezes your car
blows another tire the radiator's shot
and i a would-be bride a modern-
day Godiva i've opened my eyes
never fear Mrs. Wenderby's fire-proof heart
and the yodel shaken loose from her windpipe

time for a little fun where the epistles prosper
and thistles thrive among the oats
we would sneak out past and jump
right in front of the congregation
who watch from behind the fly-specked windows

this is where you should ask me for a dance

changelings

on the gravel road to the river
the springs in his chest pop

the allure of axle and blacktop
the hum of the motor in his ear
the window flashing down and up
mosquitoes in bloody smears

'ts the way of the world he says
we are changelings in high romance

    1. if you, not me
    2. if me, not you
    3. if not for me, who
    4. if not us

     , here we are
     , the two of us
   hot as a galloping jalapeño
   here in the changing
   room forever unchanging
   as Avogadro's number

rustlers

the skunk is a little atomizer
dead beside the road Paul dead
-sober dangling his words
from the saddle and moping
like an abandoned dog

has parcels he wants
to bring special delivery
his voice darkens
as if he were a rustler and he himself
a fugitive from love

it was time to realize, didn't i know,
his eyes turn soda-blue
when they blunder through the house
one bruiser of a fly in winter

the two of us unsure
when the match begins
        or)if it(ends
stand around like wrestlers

and we hang around some more

the sound in my heart

i grow tired and learn to listen
for the sound in my heart
or his when for a moment he holds me
and i draw back alarmed
at the loudness and knowing
one day it will go out

am a wet towel i can't get out of
other times a stray Paul stirs up
on his way to somewhere
the pony a little shaky our talk prickly

when he drinks from the dipper
he wipes his mouth with a sigh
and the back of his hand

you'd think we'd learn
that the stories wilt
like impatiens in the heat
and what doesn't blows past

every night under the big dipper
the stars feel stiff as forever
and i grow thirsty for something to say
for what i wanted to hear

she contemplates meeting

slow sounds from the cattle
a cat that yawns for
the spray of warm milk

i myself yearn for a string
that would lead me past
the gate in my head past the chicken
coop on the edge of the yard
a bright thread i would hang
a goldenrod moon from

would find you
on a twiddle of electricity

come in come in please come in
    one of us says
and we all lean in, conspiratorially
the dials wet with enormity

    listen to the fiddling and crackling
      inside the cabinet
the riddle of being there

summer fair

Paul and i go
round and round
hoping we will bump
like cars, sorry sorry
spiky grass and sun
so unforgiving it scratches

Paul determined to buy me
a hot dog *with everything*

carnival he explains is
a farewell to flesh

heard what he told me
heard what he said

the onions and the wieners sizzle
the chips sail in their salt and vinegar
how can there be any getting away
with anything or any one

  the girls pretending
   they are dizzy
     or frightened
  let themselves go
   into someone's arms

my voice high and skittish
no,no i couldn't really
Paul offering
to take me
for a ride

goin' down the road

Paul in full grin on the way
the brutal sunshine
falls in avalanche

watch him on Harlequin
leg cocked ear cocked
how foolish he is and how
much i wish him

here he comes reins in hand
so pleased with himself
he jingles & sparkles

his head jostles with words
he has carried under his arm
small parcels he
sober as a parson
has wrapped & tied
consigned them:

To: MRS. P. BENTLEY

he is delivering them in person
and they thump when he
dumps them dramatically
and i think dear god
he will slash it open

what does he think
I'm some kind of cowgirl
feckless in love
gangly with freckles

thinks he is on an adventure
i call him from but i call to him
from the steps where my marriage sits
Philip hunched under
suitcase in hand

she invites him in

still she is there
some slack in the line
she pulls him in on

Pa-aullll she says
would you
like to have a bit
with us tonight

IV.

VI

soufflenheim

keeping time or making
it's a scuffle of wind
a snuffle of smoke

Phil & Phyllis are playing
house in an earthen home
a clay pot, a breathing place

he thinks of her

maybe you are the wind
the afternoon hot & slamming
& i a broken windmill
trying to catch you from falling

except it is not
you are not
the hot prairie wind
hard & shoving

misgiving

the poplars are holding on
their shoulders at least one
black crow who yells in their ears
threatens to crack the cup
in which the unborn jiggle

she has burnt her thumb
                anxious to know
what the birds are saying
                inside the shell

fears someone will
touch her and the darkness
will break open in her hand

caesarian

the words folded
into a plain envelope
with a two-cent stamp of the king
and a ragged edge your thoughts
fall from or are taken
when i rip it open
and there is no taking back

a spot of blood
where you had cut
your tongue sealing
whatever you said
or meant to say
or thought you meant

sparrows

leaves
    you think

         —leaves

       /moving fast

   , quick , small bits

  whipt in wind

 a handful of tiny birds

       sparrows?

they seem
     smaller

  \quicker

last days

i.

    sun all day rattles
    the paths in the grass

ii.

    in some world
    a fisherman flicks
    & the spoon whizzes
        , plunk ,
    into the water

iii.

    who knows why
    when we are cast
    the sky will crack
        open &
    the sun fall out

iv.

    who can say why
    the day blows

                or why children
            fall down the stairs

prophecy

you are holding out
and the world is slithering off the road

what about the pillar of fire by night
the dust by day the dry-paper heat

how about the sun that today pulverizes our breath
what to say about our toady souls stashed in the dirt
our throats hoping for rain and swollen ditches
and for summers we can splash like ducks

i know the day eats our flesh as if it were fire
that fire goeth before stubble and burns our flesh
and we probably are virtuous
as only in deserts we can be
truer than locusts and lizards

i know we are
thirty going on thirsty
that our spirits like the wells
run dry and we grow
thrifty with salt

that the bushes turn brown & crackling
that fire runs along the ground and in the trees

knowing the word
is a fever in my bones
why would you begrudge
a little mud on my skirt

cattle in winter

the morning after
Jan 31 & 30 below
so polished with cold
you can see forever
and the joy of the foot
warmer under the robes

back from the Benson parish
Philip and i ride up
the world round us turning
stark & blue as electricity
so close everything seems
to have shut & perished

at the Harneys' rise
the runners break the crust
horses snuffling the sound
of harness so clear it could be
the beginning of the world

the day so bleak i
could weep for loneliness

i was thinking we could stop
at the Lennochs' for a cup of tea
yes Philip i would like that
that would be nice

and over the crest
the sudden sprawl

the red & white animals
a wagon, old cart,
high narrow sides /tipped

dozens of legs in the air
all those cattle frozen solid
where they drifted on storm

amaryllis

first thing in the morning
when the frost has grown up her throat
and the kettle is gasping
until it fogs the pane

she does not notice
she has been saving
and has buried the amaryllis
up to the neck in clay

the glass blooms with the sun
and she breathes on her fingers
feels the fat bulb burst and
she follows its thrust
up the long green neck

in the chill it lifts
a blood-red face
up to her

every tuesday

also thursday every thursday
and sometimes wednesdays

i hang my heart in the window
my shadow on the snow
you could see right through

would glow if
you were to hold it
up to the summer

when you warm your hands
on it you will feel
a quart-size ticking
perhaps you could
crank it up to hurricane

renunciation

had you not folded yourself into
an ecstasy of nos and nevers
and slammed the drawer shut
with nails & denials & a skeleton key
lodged between your breasts

festooned yourself in not-now's
a gainsay of knots & upbraidings

and a silver mirror in which
you cannot catch yourself
or the ghost of your want

had you not snuffed the candle
to your slow saline heart
which secretes a pearl
known only to you

here & now

what gain
against the grain
on the corner of Now
& Yet-Again St.
right next to Here
-We-Go-Again Blvd.

we hunch in a house so flimsy
it shatters with the scratch of a match

would that we were beloved
and wedded to the blue
and emerald birds who live
just outside the door
on air rubbed smooth as water

she has scanned

the wallpaper that lines her room
curtains stained with water & squashed flies

she has checked for dust &
what she has left of scars
wept for what remains of the stars
that once swept over

she runs her fingers through
the summers that had glowed at the door
and at the latch now speak

she can hear them
levitate like holy men
sent from the west

every night she turns away
to the worn scantlings of her house
the rafters her ribs have become
the trunks in which she has padlocked
her sun-dried flower

the back step

the back step, Steven and i,
Steven Philip and i, watching,
the sky's high gesture
the nights ablaze

look at the stars i want to shout
i should throw stones
into the weather
wish i knew and could tell you what

they're germs, Steven says. God sneezes
to know
and the sky's measly with germs

who can know
what they are, the stars that breathe
with their mouths wide open
but cannot tell me
where now you are

eremite

        have made my feelings
        like my hands
        dry and chapped
        so it may seem to others

strange spider i have
knit life into fluster & tangle
tucked my dreams too
like a potato into a gunny sack &
      yanked it shut

        burlap bag doesn't cut it
        my heart safe
        to say is a strong
        box lined with prudence
        and a little lead

i have been reckless
at least in reclusion
kept my treasures intact
secure from snitch
& sniff & pilfer

she rejoices in her days

my apron where it droops
in patches over the chair
is the colour of peaches

beside the iron beneath the blue porcelain
with the crack in its lip El Greco
stinking with fleas he cannot scratch
sings out as if he were a lead in the Baptist choir
the chamber pot that is chipped and broken
catches his howls and the *plink*
plink from the stains in the ceiling

Philip old owl winces when he
       blinks into the room
where i have been washing
saskatoons and chopping onions
enquiry in his eyes   or hesitation

Harlequin snorts when he jingles
to the porch and Steven
in a fistful of life

the thin lips of Mrs. E. saying no
no she doesn't and no i shouldn't
                why should i

also the thin legs of the Wenderby children
their faces when Paul pulls out the licorice

the thoughts whump past
in an apple dumpling
a well to water the world

i am the seven seas in seventh
heaven when the earth began
      to glow just now
    just a moment ago

the air strangely dead

kerosene lamp in winter
the smell of darkness
streaking the glass

smoky rope of their waiting
keeping their vigil by night

you somewhere
over the dark
possibly serene

this is in winter
this is for you
this is for what
i cannot say
this is for all
you did not say

this is for you
this is for now

the days unfold

some call it scant
the scent of a bird singing
the nearness of its belonging

but hunger arrives in a glider
and it drops into the hangar where you
have crashed and now store
your wind-torn heart

the seasons come & go
north south east west the days
something to behold
something to languish
something to puncture
your sun-burnt skin

small birds

if you touch me i will
open like a confession
a ripe plum in your mouth

every spring we fear gossips
at tea & cookies splice our wire bodies
tight & creaking
& we teeter in wind

at night we make the cries
small birds make
when they are flying

dreamt of you

the wind. and her. the two of you
against the school   coats flapping
she is saying what's wrong, what's
wrong with you? why won't you?
she has to lean close, the wind

     you wince and
               pull away

another time, two women, lissome
          their yellow
dresses billow slightly. they are
smiling they say well they are
waiting. for you. and i keep
thinking well, so am
i, i am waiting. for you

they may be lovely
and their eyes luminous
but you are going to see me,
      and we
will skew away into the rainy air

what I wanted

                    want still
someone who will barge into
my cupboard emotions

ride a painted pony right
straight up to the drink &
pull the plug, glug,

also yank open the drawers
in which i hide & sigh
a sideboard melancholy

it's not too much
to ask such favours
a masked man who could blast
holes through or at least
perforate my cardboard heart

put it in a sticky ring
binder stinging with tears
and paper flowers
that are oozing glue

she gets ideas

this is what they say the men
whose lives choke them
a harness that galls & blisters
words that scald like mustard plaster

it will go on & on & on
cold hail heat wind lightning
it's all too good for us they say

        we must wait for a garden
            wet from roses and
          noses cold with the rain

let's get on with it
can't wait for the lilies
or the lies to die
I could go for that

        it is the Dirty Thirties
        and what about ours, i could
        say that, we could try that,
        enough of the prudent
        no more burnt to charcoal

        how about a handsome caller
        what about a horse
        of a different colour
        a brighter collar
        a little horsing around

Christmas Eve

she would breathe deeply
the colour of the mid-winter moon
the smell of candle

when first they were lit
the soft yellow of Christmas Eve

the girls would enter
the chill of the room
their clear high voices
in the darkness

the fluttered lights
each of them carrying
their hands following
either side of the light
the fragrance of candle on their skin
the room beginning to breathe against the chill

dipping the fire into another hand
that lights with a small whuff
and dripping onto another
hand to hand moving the light
spreading small fire after fire
beginning to melt the winter night

the high sky outside
the stars so bright and so cold
they could hardly breathe

travelling salesman

had i not noticed
wasn't it obvious how cordial
my fuller man with the wind
he whisks around his shoulders
perfect gentleman caller

the moon a bottle of vanilla
he pulls briskly from his pocket
how could i be so oblivious
or he so obvious

didn't that tell me something
what could i say for myself

unreturned

i could
sow some bones
with the cabbage
in the back yard
put something in
to the bruised and suffering dirt

only it goes
wrong nothing comes
back to me

you have felt it
where you sway on your knees

who can tell anyone
what shall be after
them under the sun
how can one be
warm alone
or take the chill from the stars

voilà

a bird whirrs & whirrs
  in her neck

wish i could   tell you
      what it is
with me   at home she says

    her voice papery
    hardly   there

windflowers

a film of snow
and little fires under

     like Christ
waiting to happen
waiting to break
through the crust

crocus shivering in the wind
bruises in the dusty grass

when they poke through
their mouths open wide
you wonder are they
blue from hurt or
blue from the cold

Closed Until Further Notice

he decides my soul is derelict
unfrequented as a banker's heart

that's his complaint and that
i could be a little more
compliant a little more
forthcoming surely
that and if it's ok with me
a little less complaisant

     why head straight to the cemetery
         when the gate drags open
           on grit and weathered wood

sees me as a trapdoor he will fall through
like a ruined troubadour
or a highway man caught in a heist

as if the room were booby-trapped
and it slams suddenly shut
a place where somebody
has posted a notice
Closed Until Further Notice

v.

small laugh

her voice searching
hello she says and waves
a rake-slim woman
bright eyes, tremulous
her hair is warm and brown,
unsure what i might think

Philip holds himself against speaking
something he perhaps can hear
in her quick and breathy song

a woman wondering what
          he might
               say or she
          would do
touches her throat

killdeer

the high cries of distress
kil-dee kil-dee
a quick off-kilter run
i try to follow

skitters and   pauses
she is dragging a wing
like a burden, a flutter

leads me from the
shallow scrape in the ground
lined with pebbles
and four eggs
beige and speckled black

the small flowers

at night she lays
   awake   \listening

      she will sit up and she
     will remember the grass was spikey
       the small flowers shaken
         out of the wind
      in yellow & blue spots & white
       the dust of their perfume

       on the top of the world
        the sky scudding

bearing your name

want to hold it against me
more than anything
not seeing you
    not saying

the woman at the store
says you are
a lonely man. for sure,
balky she says.
                  right there.

and everyone would see
you and me in my calico life
a few cracked teacups and
a handful of yellowed doilies

and the feeling of
all over again

pebbles

work the small stones in my hand
and worry what is stored in them

the brown ones are small
and reassuring in the palm
and some so coarse i squeeze them
and some i worry to know they're real

and the one in my apron
is so smooth and so shining
it clicks in the dark

hold them close
as my thoughts of you
familiar as an old penny
washed from the pocket
or button torn from a shirt

not much of you left but
something hard as a pebble
and i rub what i have kept
the memory bright
as a brand-new dime

we draw our breath

to say we are huers of would
drawers of if and who's-to-say
we spend our winters under glass
draw our breath as if we were artisans
and polished our thoughts
clear as water from the well

saved them up for the four angels
standing at the far corners of the earth

concert

in the evening the light
dissolves what held
the day in place
and we tune the set to
the soft and dusty voice

     when i click on
the small light i can see the dress
the fine crochet shining
the thrill you feel inside
so close to somewhere

     lean into the whiff
strange as someone in France
who gathers honey and
a happy yellow music
and once someone husky as Garbo
when it comes into the room
you can hear the voices all night

sometimes they have a long black stick
in a cabinet and somewhere behind
people growl and yell in other rooms
ditzy tunes in mellow voices
you never heard

at the end the box speaks softly
into the darkness carries the voices
and the music into the night

in what of you

her dark friend on the other side
declares in a confident voice
men are afraid of women

and the fair-haired woman
turns in a laugh
so tell me she says
the fine hair on her neck shining
the woman of freckles and laughter
leans further and her eyes
in a quick light leave their hiding

something in her voice is saying
or wanting to say
i do not know
why you are here
or why it pleases me
that you are

she poses

something caught
and can not move
could not say
a thing
all i could think
him and me and the pebbles
stick to my fingers
and i know she hears
the storm in my throat

you should come over
some time she says
you don't know how much
Philip thinks of you

all i can think is the train huffing
past or over and the two of us
flooded with loneliness
him and me outside the glass
and listening

and times in the room
when he brushes
my nipples darken
his hand shadows
every hill and fold
anyone can see

all i can think is pebbles
i have pebbles in my mouth

proðigal of ðream

the nights hold
the lights of distant cities
and trains loom out of the dark
and careen past in a spray of embers

and we watch lanterns that
sway past in the windows

look at this he says look at this
and I see in the glass looking back
          it is her heart
a small suitcase to somewhere

radio active

their fingers burn
with what is in their head
from what they have heard
from what they have touched
and what they dared

thinking to snuff and
stuff the voices back
into the wooden box

the anger of angels
the danger of the box
dark luminosities
glowing by the bed

Judith

a gray doubt in her eyes
fragile as a broken wing
when she pumps and turns
her feet on the way scuffing
leans back and swoops
        the air lifts
the dress around her
    laughs when she
feels herself rising
and falling through air

loves the feel of
her legs in the air
rising and falling
hair blowing
the wind in her face
swung like a bird
torn off the earth

the feel in her stomach
when she holds and
lets go the earth
drops out beneath her

the moment when
she lands in a skid
and a quick nervous run

snowblind on a siding

did you ever feel Jude
you had lost your right
side left your life behind
snowblind and sitting on a siding

the train uncaring as a bay street lawyer
is side-winding off to somewhere
wet and huffy and definitely panting
      definitely important

it also stops
at a hitching with grit in its eye
an enormous animal panting at the stations
it has chased itself for hundreds of miles
to catch its breath and to take
down water in great loud gulps

the train would heave
its shadow onto the snow
and over the platform leave it
full of cold and freight and you
alone and waiting

the land in all directions
wherever you look
is beautiful and empty
not a footprint in sight

missing person

*

let me in. let me in

i could live

in the

places you keep

*

this is for you
she said
i made it myself

a cup
still warm from her hand

i would like you
to have it she said

*

a small chill in the air
the windy night
about to ignite
the hairs on her arm
alive & listening

heard him
turn away
with a click
close the door
softly behind

*

wished he could swim
the warm estuaries of her love

a place so new
they would pass through
without knowing
an old way of grieving

as if they were
under water breathing
in & out together

*

when
you are here
there now will be

all that
now we were
when then was now
& there was here

when you speak
this is when
this is after
just before

this then

*

at night
there is
some
one in
my head

no
one in
my bed

*

when you
stand and
reach out

the blood rushes
the legs you
left behind

you try to
     stand
    hands out
  awkward
    as if
  holding
back the wind

*

can you hear
    where ever you are
  when you
lie awake
all night & listen

whatever you do
  can you hear me
at night
    thinking of you

VI.

IV

a hurricane of wind

there can be no surcease from
the *whOO-sshhh*
that blew up my dress
blew up my dreams
and swept them open

as i knew it could
as i hoped it might
as i thought of yes
i knew i would

all the what-ifs and you-bets
riffled my dress open

came as a one-legged thief in the night
the air crackling like candy wrapper

i was pining for a warm breath
for baring wetness
swimming with Jesus

the pebbles clack

such a thin thing
when she dings the pebbles
what could she be thinking
amidst ladies armed with spoons that ding
and stains that ring the cups

her small breasts
when the wind presses and she
out of breath says perhaps she might
call me
one time

when i hear it
in her breaking
their faces alarmed and
looking at each other
her words fall into my ear
the sounds of clicking
against the window

she bides her time

the shadows spread like burnt sugar
i have rubbed off the sun i am
a chantarelle or at least a bulb
about to grow inside the room
a cool, dry, dark place

no wild-rose smirk from me
i plan to squeeze
the cold out like toothpaste
wear it as glossy lipstick
and glow in the dark

all winter i gladden
with thoughts of glamour
the naked lady in Amsterdam
or at least a ballerina in Moscow

i warm to the idea of being an am
aryllis who all of a sudden
in a sneeze wakens
red-faced in the dark

skittish

       when you stand near
the corner of Exact Excitement and About
-Time Blvd you're not far
from the intersection of
    Exit & Forgetit

impossible to scoop Sunday off the floor
in a Schottische and a pile of sawdust
we stoop in a house so flimsy
it shatters with the scratch of a match

would that we were beloved
as were Mr. Adam and Ms. Upand
At'em wedded to the blue

end of the day

a long low light
i am burning dry

a warm animal
you can smell, close,
sends pale & fumbling feelers

Philip at the window
is thinking
I have stepped
into the dark shed the day
hot & itchy at my feet

in the back Nellie
looks up,
shifts & rubs
what am I doing here

a thick placenta
i could choke and die in

if it is true

the gate is hung on the wind
and our lives no less

who can imagine
the man in the furnace
when they crank the door open
and there he is
what must they have said and
how may we hope, on fire

at night he will emerge
in dreams so ponderous
we will squat in plain brown pots
rough to the hand and
waiting to levitate

just the two of us in the rose
garden tacky with nectar

our voices will make the sounds of water
and tea the colour of cinnamon

she hides her face

your thoughts glued
in shadows to the floor
make a tearing sound
when they pull them
looking for something spiders
might have spilled

nothing easy as drawing
gold from straw or peeling
bandages from a tacky heart
that leave a dirty film behind

when you push aside the curtains
something in the darkness almost touches
the life you have warmed in a locket

a strange intimate cry
the small birds calling
sweetness sweetness sweetness

she is wounded

i wish
more than anything
something for
her gray-blue eyes

may she learn to love
the bitter winds that blow
out of my mouth

and the tangle of burrs
i have gathered for her red hair

most of all
the fingernail i have kept
for the milky blue in her eyes

somewhere near Campman

        a stable in fall
the tall smell of horses
softness of their mouths
their long yellow teeth

her face a monsoon
dives into the light
the lamp lets out
issue issue issue it says

the moon in its
boney face watches
her nearness to the lamp
its swollen throat
the round black tongue

when she undoes the buttons
one by one she listens to
        the sounds of
            her breathing

her breasts white as the winter moon
) as round
above the darkness of her body

wouldn't stop

held them and counted
the small glasses on the tray
that said something sweet
and a stronger smell in the yard
tar and grasshoppers

he was 39 or 40
she 32 or so and so

when they scratched at the door
they did not want to step into the cold
where the train slid by swoosh
scraping the grit so close
they could have been
caught in the draught
left like a burp after dinner

when they climbed the fence
and carried themselves through the weeds
into the ravine they took
their fervor down to the frogs
that screamed all night
a light-headedness in the mud
and to what all summer
they had feared and hoped

wishedtheycould wishedtheycould
the wheels go   on and on and
wouldn'tstop wouldn'tstop
                    wouldn't stop

the itch

when we felt the hard need for something
we swam in the ditches

plums once plump with flesh
and skins that were duskily shining
had turned into thorns and dry rubber
as if the stones were torn out

overtaken by the scabrous days of summer
and algae clogging the sloughs
   "the itch" we call it
   it gets into the blood
   gets under your skin

  the smart so strong
  you cannot shake it

for their needs are strong

that we may love one another
we must forget the daffodils
the perky stash of tulips
you will hand me in the spring
same for the lilacs by the pump
and the small puddles
     sparrows dip
  their tiny thirst in

you can maketh me to lay
down among the stooks and in the hay
loft for our needs are strong
asketh me to wait
in windows on windy prairies
when the door crashes shut
for here at the best of times
     are we saved

    such beloved is the fly
    mired on a curling ribbon
    life buzzing out of its side

        so also the boys who cling
        like flies to the screen door
          & none of them know
          what they are doing
          or why they are there

under the trestle

i hang the lantern in my heart
turn it up until it hisses brightly
and he can see it swaying

before he takes & tips it
in the shed by the track

    i will be burning smokily
      when he leans
        across to
      blow it out

but not until we have found
under the eye that thunders
across the trestle
a small wet answer

they meet in the night

it is raining
and she is running
past the grocery store past
the livery past lives
they are delivered from

the elevators erect and red
-faced resist caring

Judith Judith he calls
dropping into the ravine
wind and rain all over

the trestle shaking
the big body
whoofing through the night

their white faces are looking out,
and she loses her footing

cold rain
the night jerking
open and closed

the big bright eye
the windows full of eyes

they meet in rain

run out of the lightning
hard rain on the roof
and the dog barking

you are here she says
dark water in her eyes
a small laugh
you have come
she has found me

her hands
heavy and rain
a cold face

there and there.   and here.
her eyes dark
yes she says yes yes

on the other side
faces blurred in rain
until we no longer care

her mouth a pocket of warmth

the weight of our clothes

wide awake all spring,
  the night cries
    land on our ears

trace the black vein along the tracks
  the path round as a hip
    we are sliding into the ravine
      the muddy banks

the smell of water
  and then we hear it
    feel the heaviness

    carrying us to the bottom
to the cattails where they are broken and pilling
      your hand cold on my face
  the dumbness of buttons
    and the close and sudden warmth
breasts touching mouth tongue nipple
    until i must lie down

clothes snagging on the way back
  we are dragging ourselves
    as if we have come from sleep

want that

to dance in jubilation
on a Saturday night

         not only that
      but that\
        /that too

    the endless fib
   rillations our own jeopardy

when the sun crashes
through the screen door
and skedaddles over the horizon

i want the reckless hearts
overturned with a clatter
bowling pins, only louder

recital

     heretofore a pinafore threatening
      to pop the buttons i am now
       a piano in a dance band

    and now the two of us
bare-footed on the patio
     ooo ooOO *O O O*
doing the foxtrot the rhumba the tango
the potato and the cabbage
my heart slaps)who cares(
like a screen door in a big wind

in an anise night
we will make music until
the morning arises and the sun
promises to rinse off the mud
to iron out the creases
smooth all our wrinkles away

alas alas we will sing
sea chanteys sail at last
through arias & chansons
fling cherubs and spiders
sticky lines across the atlas

everyone will hear the grasshoppers
HUZZAH HUZZAH

my heart will go
WHUMP
clink clink go
the keys to my heart

copyrighted

forget it they say
   how can
   we write
our dreams on an outbuilding
   a huge perforated disk
      finger tip to shoulder

LOVE IN A DRY LAND

   it says   nailed to the inner wall
   we can hear it hiss & click
   it skitters & ticks & scratches
   a small opera of voices

Copyrighted by the Regina Music Box Co 1897 love they say
   cannot be done
   nor is it heard
   is not to be
read or spoken
who can believe
   or take joy in

love that is
the thin needle
the same old tune
circular with yearning
kiss it says kiss kiss
in our heads it goes
round & round
and will not
stop

I am grateful for Turnstone's continuing support of love in a dry land *and for Rob Budde's thoughtful editing of the book.*